OCS Report
MMS 2007–045

Investigation of Fatal Accident Lift Boat-Coil Tubing P&A Main Pass Block 98, Well No. 3 OCS-G 5694 12 August 2005

I0410929

Gulf of Mexico
Off the Louisiana Coast

Jack Williams – Chair
Leslie Peterson
Kirk Malstrom

U.S. Department of the Interior
Minerals Management Service
Gulf of Mexico OCS Regional Office

New Orleans
July 2007

Contents

Recommendations

List of Figures

Investigation and Report

Authority

A fatal accident (the Accident) occurred on 12 August 2005 at approximately 0012 hours aboard the lift boat *Myrtle*, contracted to Forest Oil Corporation (Operator) while plug and abandon (P&A) operations were being conducted for the Operator on Lease OCS-G 5694, Main Pass Block 98, Well No. 3 (the Well), in the Gulf of Mexico, offshore the State of Louisiana. The fatally injured person was a crew member for a coil tubing unit (CTU) from Coil Tubing Services (CTS or the CT Contractor).

Pursuant to Section 208, Subsection 22 (d), (e), and (f), of the Outer Continental Shelf (OCS) Lands Act, as amended in 1978, and Department of the Interior Regulations 30 CFR 250, Minerals Management Service (MMS) is required to investigate and prepare a public report of this Accident (the Investigation). By memorandum dated 18 August 2005, and revised 18 January, 2006, the following personnel were named to the investigative panel (the Panel):

Jack Williams, Chairman – Office of Safety Management, Field Operations, GOM OCS Region;
Leslie Peterson – Houma District, Field Operations, GOM OCS Region;
Kirk Malstrom – Regulations and Standards Branch, OMM, Herndon.

Procedures

On the morning of 12 August 2005, two representatives from the Department of the Interior, Minerals Management Service (MMS) District Office in New Orleans, Louisiana, visited the site of the Accident to assess the situation, take photos and statements, and gather information. On 16 August, a member of the Panel took part in a meeting with Operator's personnel to review the Operator's post-accident proposed changes in procedure. On 1 February 2006, members of the Panel met and reviewed documents, pictures, and written accounts of the Accident. On 8 March 2006, the Panel reviewed the data received and organized the lines of inquiry of the Investigation. On 2 June 2006, the Panel met and reviewed the findings of the Investigation, and agreed on what additional information was needed. Other data were acquired by the Panel and used in the course of the Investigation, including information from interviews, telephone conferences and other meetings, and various documents provided by the companies and regulatory agencies involved in the Investigation.

The Panel also met, discussed the evidence, and reviewed progress of the Investigation on a number of occasions. After having considered all of the information available, the Panel produced this report.

Introduction

Background

Lease OCS-G 5694 covers approximately 5,000 acres and is located in Main Pass Block 98 (MP-98 or the Lease), Gulf of Mexico, off the Louisiana Coast *(for lease location, see figure 1)*. The Lease was originally purchased and operated by Corpus Christi Exploration on behalf of several partners. In 1983, the initial well was drilled, and the Lease was placed on production in 1986. Beginning in 1994, the Lease passed though a variety of ownership consortiums and operators. Forest Oil Corporation acquired majority interest and became designated operator in 2001. Cumulative drilling on the lease resulted in a total of 13 completions, 6 of which produced at various times.

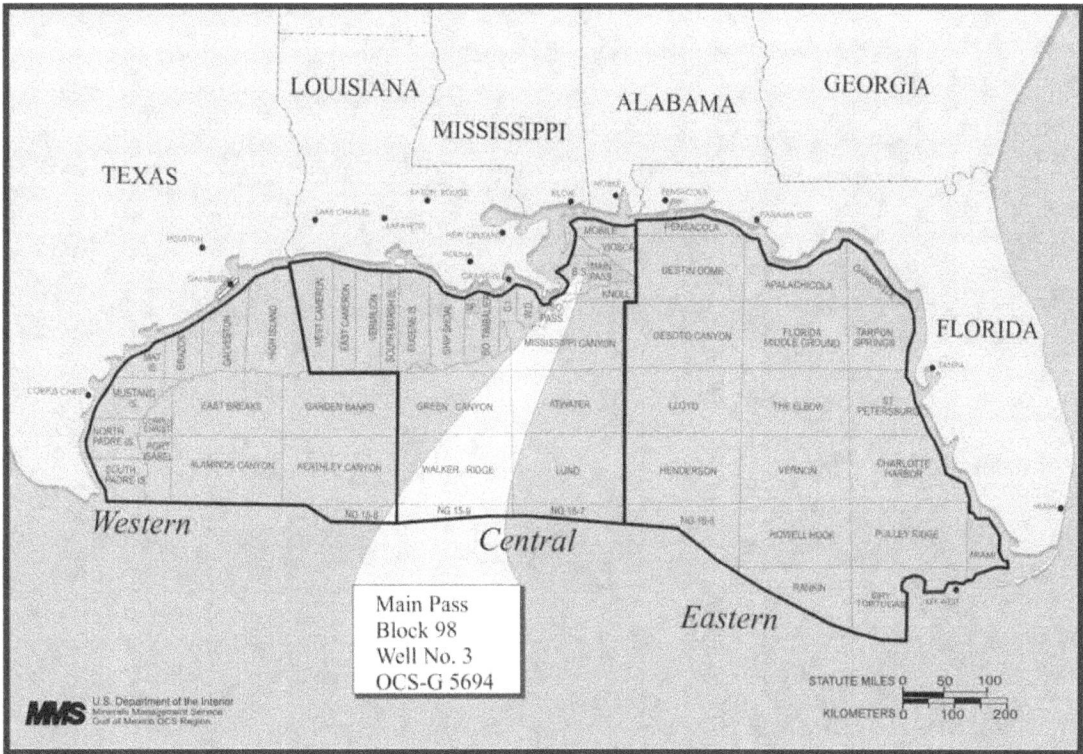

Figure 1: Location of Lease OCS-G 5694, Main Pass Block 98, Well No. 3

In July 2004, the long string of the subject well was producing gas and was the only producing well on the Lease. Production ceased in September 2004 as a result of Hurricane Ivan, when the hurricane caused the well conductor caisson to be bent almost level with the seafloor, destroying the platform. The Operator announced plans to drill a replacement well in 2005 to hold the lease, but the well was ultimately cancelled. In 2005, the Operator decided to P&A the Well. The last Oil and Gas Operations Report (OGOR) was received in December 2005, and the Lease was terminated on 30 September 2006.

Brief Description, Fatality on Lift Boat

On 11-12 August 2005, operations to P&A the subject Well were continuing on the modified lift boat, *Myrtle* (the Lift Boat). To P&A the bent well, the caisson and casing had been cut below the mud line (BML) and tie-back tubing strings had been attached to the 2⅜-inch production tubing. The tie-back strings were secured by slips into a tubing holding device,

Figure 2: Lift boat, extension platform

the "False Rotary" or "Slip Bowl," mounted on a temporarily constructed extension deck

Figure 3: False rotary or slip bowl and BOP assembly

platform (the Extension Platform) attached to the bow of the Lift Boat *(see figure 2)*. A coil tubing unit was being rigged up on one of the tie-back strings above the Slip Bowl, preparatory to washing mud and testing the tie-back overshot connection.

Approximately at 0012 hrs, 12 August 2005, after the CTU Blowout Preventor (BOP) stack and other equipment (the BOP Assembly) had been installed, the crane was disconnected from the BOP Assembly in preparation for the next lift in the CTU rig-up operation. The boat was felt to shake and the CTU BOP Assembly swayed. Then the tubing to which the CTU BOP Assembly was attached bent sharply. The CTU BOP Assembly broke free and fell overboard *(see figure 3)*. A CTU technician (CT Tech) sitting on top of the CTU BOP Assembly and attached to that assembly by fall protection restraints was pulled into the Gulf of Mexico by his fall protection harness.

A diver was jumped within 13 minutes of the incident and located the CTU BOP Assembly on the seafloor. The CT Tech was freed from the CTU BOP's and raised to the Lift Boat deck within 45 minutes of the Accident. Life support first aid was performed on the CT Tech for approximately one hour, but the CT Tech did not respond. First aid was ceased at approximately 0145 hrs upon receipt of verbal concurrence of Coast Guard personnel.

An autopsy ruling of drowning as the cause of death was completed 12 August 2005 at 1300 hrs. The autopsy was performed by Jefferson Parish Coroner in Harvey.

Findings

Situation Prior to Operations

Well History

Figure 4: MP-98 Well #3, pre Hurricane Ivan

The Well was drilled from a three-well production platform set in 78 ft of water in 1986 and completed as a dual well with two strings of 2 ⅜-inch production tubing, the "long string" (LS) and the "short string" (SS). In 1998, Hurricane George damaged the platform to the extent that two of the three producing wells on it were P&A'd with only the #3 Well being salvaged. On the #3 Well, the drive pipe was bent by the storm, but was straightened somewhat by using a derrick barge. A large overdrive caisson (the Caisson) was installed but found to be skewed. After two pin piles and braces straightened the Caisson to acceptable standards, production decks were welded on the Caisson and production equipment was spotted on the decks (*see figure 4*).

Prior to Hurricane Ivan, the Well was producing 1 to 2 million cubic feet of gas per day (mmcfd) on the LS from a sand slightly deeper than 5,000 ft. The SS had ceased production some months earlier and was thought to be possibly sand plugged. Some casing pressure was evident on the annulus of the production-surface casing.

In September 2004, Hurricane Ivan tracked through the Caribbean and Central Gulf of Mexico for over two weeks before the eye came ashore at Gulf Shores, Ala., on 17 September 2004.

The MMS estimated that 150 platforms were in the direct path of Hurricane Ivan. Industry reported to MMS that seven platforms were destroyed and six platforms had major damage. One of the destroyed platforms was the Main Pass Block 98 Well No. 3 Caisson. Hurricane Ivan toppled and bent the Caisson and casing almost flat onto the ocean floor (*see figure 5*).

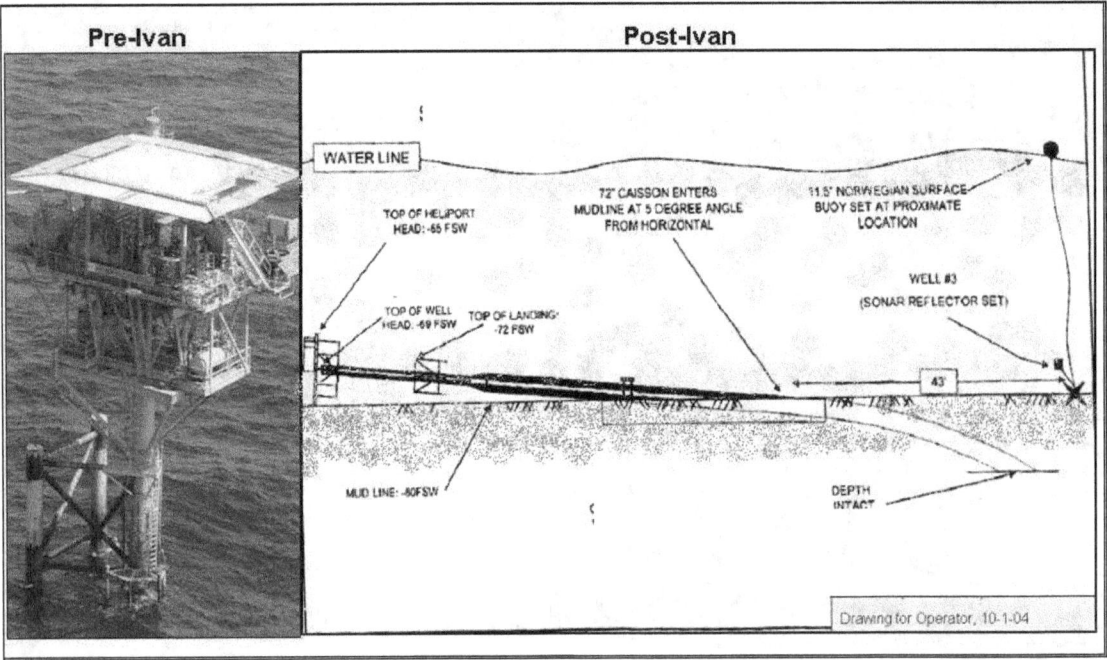

Figure 5: Main Pass 98, Well # 3 caisson, pre-Ivan, post-Ivan

An Operator survey of the damage sustained to the Well found the Caisson bent but intact as it entered the mud line at a 5-degree angle from horizontal. By jetting down to 9 ft below the mudline (BML), it was determined that the Caisson was probably intact with no buckles or tears. No gas bubbles were observed, which was interpreted as indicating that the downhole safety valves were containing well pressure.

Analysis of the post-Hurricane Ivan damage surveys caused the Operator to determine that the Well could possibly cause an uncontrolled flow of hydrocarbons should the surface controlled subsurface safety valve(s) (SCSSV) fail. As it was thought to be impracticable to repair the bent Caisson, the Operator decided to P&A the Well in a manner consistent with the regulations.

Preliminary Activities

Well Plan

To prepare for the P&A of the Well, the Operator initiated a lengthy analysis and planning process. Evaluation of the Well's condition and subsequent changes to the P&A plan (the Plan) continued through June 2005. It was determined that the SCSSV's were not leaking. However, trial attempts indicated it would be difficult to P&A the Well through the production tubing inside the bent Caisson. Attempts to access the production tubing through the bent Caisson failed when the both strings of production tubing were found to be possibly blocked by mud and sand about 10-ft BML. Because of the severity of the bend and some possible shallow casing communication problems, washing the production tubing at the extreme horizontal angle was not attempted.

By early 2005, it was calculated that the bend in the Caisson straightened to near vertical about 25 ft BML. At that time, the casing was tested and interpreted to be leak-free at that depth. The Operator's plan for P&A of the Well then developed over a number of months. The final Plan and Procedure was submitted and approved in June 2005, and proposed the following steps:

(1) Remove the platform and debris from the ocean bottom.

(2) Jet a pit around the Well to the depth where the Caisson straightened, about 25 ft BML.

(3) Cut off the entire Caisson/Well, including all casing strings and the two production tubing strings, using a diver-guided outside diamond cutter.

(4) Recover the bent portion of the Caisson and the cut casing, tubing, etc.

(5) Lower two 2 ⅜-in tubing tie-back strings from a jack-up lift boat. Each tie-back string of tubing was to be approximately 140 ft in length, and each was to be equipped with a special packoff overshot.

(6) Use a diver to guide the packoff overshots on the end of the two tie-back strings into place within the Caisson stub, and securely attach the overshots to the tops of the two production tubing strings.

(7) Once the tie-back string overshots were securely attached to the production tubing, the tie-back strings were to be placed in 5,000-lb tension and hung off in the Slip Bowl. The connection and seal between tie back and production tubing were to be confirmed and pressure tested *(see figure 6)*.

In this manner, it was planned that access to the inside of the production tubing strings would be gained, allowing the tubing to be cleared of obstructions by using wireline and a CTU, to a depth where cement could be pumped to P&A the well per regulations.

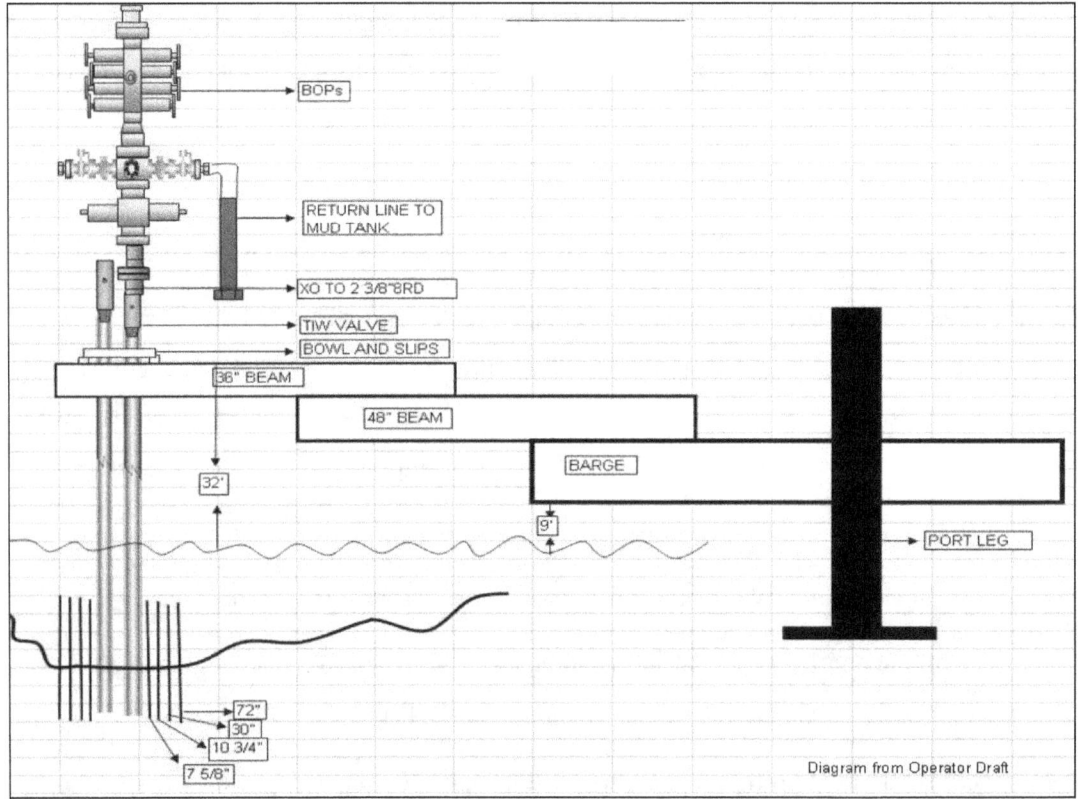

Figure 6: Diagram of lift boat, tie-back tubing, well head

Lift Boat

Because of the distance from the edge of the pit jetted into the seafloor to the center line of the Caisson, a special rig was required. Testimony indicated that most jack-up workover rigs would not be able to skid a derrick out far enough to reach the Well and keep the rig legs out of the pit jetted around the well.

The Operator assigned a Completion Engineer (CE) to design the Plan to P&A the Well and to solve the problem of direct vertical access to the Well. The CE spent considerable time solving the access problem. The solution approved by Operator review was to attach an extended temporary work platform (Extension Platform) to the bow of a large lift boat *(see figure 7)*.

The end of the Extension Platform was equipped with a False Rotary, or Slip Bowl, to hold the tie back tubing in tension. The Lift Boat selected was equipped with two cranes, one of which was "oversized"

Figure 7: Extension platform, CTU injection head

[testimony] with a boom long enough to reach over the well center at the end of the Extension Platform. This crane acted in lieu of the traveling block of a conventional rig.

The design of the Extension Platform included a safety factor and, according to documentation, its failure point was calculated to be twice the maximum loads that were anticipated to be placed on it. The CE used a number of outside specialty service company resources while developing that design. The plan for the actual P&A operation included a written procedure to be followed after the Lift Boat was on site. Shortly after the Plan design and procedure were drafted, the CE left the employ of the Operator.

From testimony, prior to the Operator finalizing the Plan, the Coast Guard notified the Operator that the Lift Boat would not be allowed to sail with the Extension Platform installed. Therefore, some additional time was spent ensuring that the Extension Platform could be constructed to engineering specifications on the Lift Boat's bow after it was jacked-up on location.

After the departure of the CE from Operator's employ, the Plan details were finished by the Completions Engineering Manager (CEM) of the Operator's drilling organization, reviewed and approved by the Operator, and submitted to MMS for approval. MMS approval was granted in June 2005. The CEM then assigned a contract offshore operations supervisor (the Company Man) to oversee the actual operation and to deal with whatever contingencies were encountered on the job. In early July, the Lift Boat moved on location and operations commenced.

Operations

Operations Prior to CTU Rig-Up

- The seafloor was jetted down to a point where the Caisson was close to vertical. Approximate depth of the hole was 25 ft; radius of the hole was estimated at 37 ft.

- The Caisson, casing, and all strings of tubing were cut externally at seafloor minus 25 ft. This left the Caisson, all casing and tubing strings flush, including the 7⅝-in production casing, and two 2⅜-in tubing production strings.

- The Lift Boat moved on location. The Extension Platform containing the False Rotary was installed to extend over the top of the Well.

- Two 2⅜-inch N80 tubing strings (tie-back strings), each approximately 140 ft in length, were made up and equipped with overshots and packoff assemblies. Supported by a crane and with a diver to guide the overshots, the tie-back strings were attached to the two production tubing strings inside the Caisson and passed through the False Rotary. Projections were welded onto the outside of the Caisson stub, and the tie-back strings were chained down to it. The tie-back strings were then put in 500-lb tension (not 5,000 lbs as recommended) and hung off in the False Rotary by slips.

11 August 0900: CT equipment and crew contracted from the CT Contractor arrived at the Lift Boat. This crew consisted of separate day and night shifts, each with a supervisor and three crew members. CTU shift change was scheduled for 0600 and 1800 hrs. The CTU and other equipment were offloaded and the night shift went to quarters.

The CTU supervisors observed working conditions on the Extension Platform to be unsatisfactory for coil tubing operations. The ends of the tie-back strings topped by the Texas Iron Works (TIW) valves were over 30 ft above the False Rotary. No hand rails were installed on the Extension Platform and large openings were present around the False Rotary.

After meeting with the Company Man and discussing the work conditions, the Slip Bowls were shimmed and H-beams and angle iron were installed to support the False Rotary and prevent its movement independent of the motion of the Lift Boat. Some grating was installed to reduce the size of open holes around the False Rotary. A wire rope hand rail was installed. A joint of tubing was removed from each tie-back string and the Lift Boat was re-positioned so that the end connections of the tie-back string assemblies were approximately 3.5 ft above the slips. The TIW valves were re-installed atop both tie-back tubing strings.

11 August 1300 hrs: The Company Man held a pre-job safety meeting. Attendance did not include the CT Contractor night shift, the night shift crane operator, and others. The written agenda did not include discussion of CTU rig-up procedure.

1530 hrs: Wireline was rigged up on one of the tie-back strings. When rig-up was completed, a gauge was run to 367 ft and the tie-back string was tested with 500 pounds-per-square-inch (psi) pressure. The tubing pressure was found to bleed to 150 psi in three seconds. Diver inspection revealed bubbles coming from around the top of the overshot/production tubing connection, indicating the packoff elements in the overshot were not holding pressure.

1800 hrs: Wireline operations continued. The wireline was rigged down on one tie-back string, and then rigged up on the other tie-back string preparatory to testing that string for blockage and its ability to hold pressure. The CTU day shift went off duty (tower). Wireline completed rigging up and a gauge ring was run into the tie-back string to approximately the top of the Caisson stub. The tubing was found to be blocked by mud at that point. It was decided to wash the mud out of the tubing by using the CTU and the wireline unit was rigged down.

2130 hrs: The Company Man found the CTU night shift supervisor and told him to begin rigging up the CTU.

Operations through the Accident

2130 hrs 12 August – 0012 hrs 13 August:

- The CTU night shift began to rig up the CTU by installing all the well control equipment (the BOP Assembly).

- An 8-round thread by flange crossover was installed.

- A 10,000-psi rated manual gate valve was installed (made up) on top of the crossover.

- The CTU BOP stack was hoisted into place and made up to the rest of the previously installed BOP Assembly *(See figure 8)*.

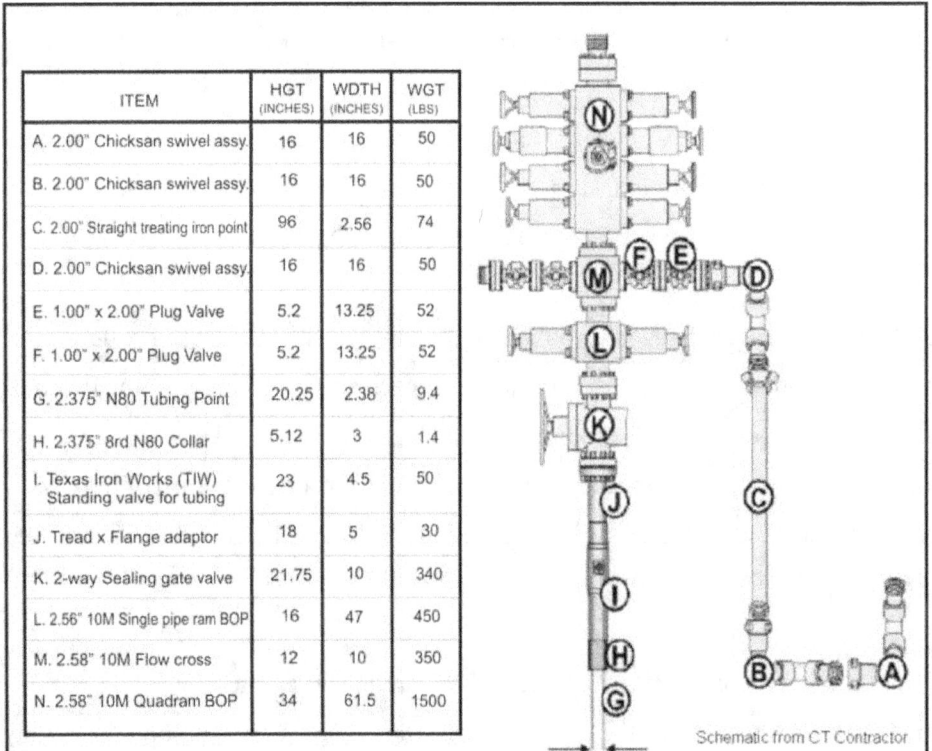

ITEM	HGT (INCHES)	WDTH (INCHES)	WGT (LBS)
A. 2.00" Chicksan swivel assy.	16	16	50
B. 2.00" Chicksan swivel assy.	16	16	50
C. 2.00" Straight treating iron point	96	2.56	74
D. 2.00" Chicksan swivel assy.	16	16	50
E. 1.00" x 2.00" Plug Valve	5.2	13.25	52
F. 1.00" x 2.00" Plug Valve	5.2	13.25	52
G. 2.375" N80 Tubing Point	20.25	2.38	9.4
H. 2.375" 8rd N80 Collar	5.12	3	1.4
I. Texas Iron Works (TIW) Standing valve for tubing	23	4.5	50
J. Tread x Flange adaptor	18	5	30
K. 2-way Sealing gate valve	21.75	10	340
L. 2.56" 10M Single pipe ram BOP	16	47	450
M. 2.58" 10M Flow cross	12	10	350
N. 2.58" 10M Quadram BOP	34	61.5	1500

Schematic from CT Contractor

Figure 8: Coil tubing BOP assembly

- The CT Tech and CTU night supervisor got a ladder and erected it next to the BOP Assembly.

- The CT Tech climbed the ladder and failed in an attempt to unscrew the lift cap from the top of the BOP Assembly.

- The CT Tech was given tools and then climbed to the top of BOP Assembly, hooked his fall protection lanyard to it and, while sitting on the top of the BOP Assembly, loosened and unscrewed the lift cap.

- The CT supervisor closed all the valves on the flow cross.

- The crane was attached and the lift cap was hoisted from the top of BOP Assembly. The CT Tech guided the cap away from BOP Assembly. The crane lowered the lift cap to the Lift Boat deck and the CTU night supervisor unhooked the lift cap. Another CTU crew member, (the Assistant) climbed partly up the ladder. The Assistant retrieved tools from the CT Tech and then held the ladder to assist the descent of the CT Tech.

- The Crane began to traverse into position to lift the CTU injector head.

- The Extension Platform, ladder, and BOP Assembly were felt to shake side to side, and the BOP Assembly began to lean over to starboard.

- The CT supervisor told the CT Tech to disconnect his fall protection from the BOP Assembly quickly and descend. The CT supervisor then turned to signal the crane to reconnect to the BOP Assembly.

- The BOP Assembly rapidly leaned to starboard, projecting over the side of the Extension Platform. The BOP Assembly broke free of the tie-back tubing string at the top of the TIW valve, and fell into the water, dragging the CT Tech, who was still connected to the BOP assembly by his fall protection harness, with it. The Assistant was struck by the treating chicksan pipe, which broke away from the BOP Assembly as it fell overboard (see figure 9). He was also thrown overboard.

- Rescue operations commenced.

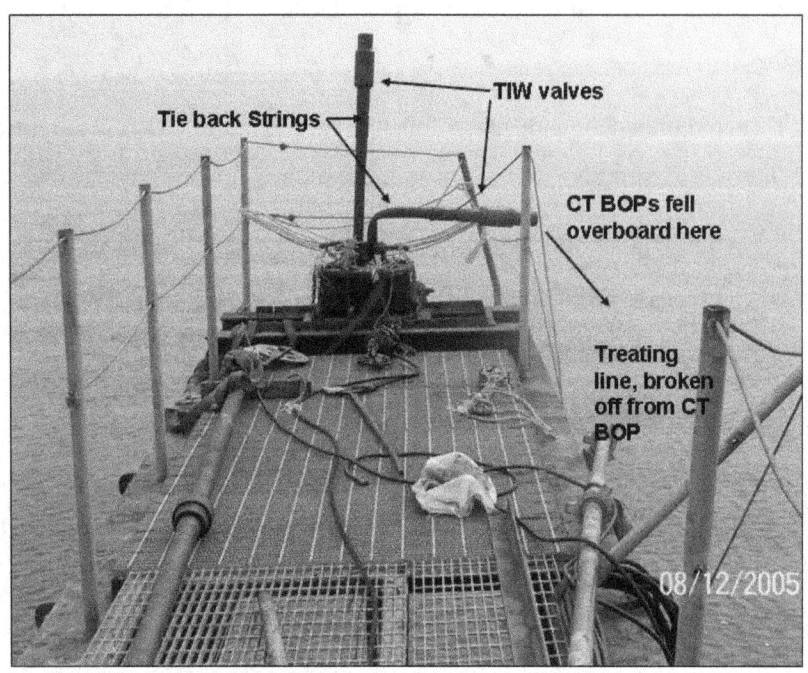

Figure 9: Extension platform after accident

Rescue Operations and Post-Accident Medical Procedures

Rescue operations were initiated, supervised by the Company Man. The Coast Guard and Medivac were called and mobilized. The Assistant was rescued from the water. Within 13 minutes a diver was awakened, equipped, and jumped to attempt a rescue of the CT Tech. The CT Tech was located by the diver, released from the BOP Assembly, and brought to surface within 45 minutes of the accident.

First aid, compression, and defibrillation were begun. Life support first aid was halted approximately one hour after the incident, after Coast Guard personnel notified the Company Man that the situation was beyond help. Later that day, the initial investigation by the MMS inspectors and others acquired pictures of the scene, written statements from key personnel, and other training, inspection, and operational information.

Personnel and Companies

The Operator personnel conducting analysis, salvage, preparation of the well site, and operations to P&A the Well were from two internal Operator organizations with separate reporting responsibilities. All rig work, lift boat and specialty operations employing snubbing units and coil tubing, etc., including all P&A's, workovers, re-completions, through-tubing re-completions, etc., are the responsibility of the Operator's Completions department, reporting through the Drilling organization in Denver. Separately, the Production office in Lafayette plans and conducts all production maintenance operations such as using wireline to gather bottomhole pressures, cutting paraffin, etc. The analysis of the Well, cleanup of the Hurricane Ivan damage, and salvage of the platform were conducted by the Production department. The decision to P&A the Well and the planning and conducting of that operation were the responsibility of the Drilling department.

Testimony indicated the CE who developed the original plan had a minimum of 10 years' experience and had designed several P&A well plans for the Operator. Testimony indicated the CEM had approximately 30 years' experience, mostly in drilling and completion operations. After the CE left the employ of the Operator a few weeks before the P&A commenced, the CEM assigned the Company Man to review and oversee the operation. Prior to that time, the CEM was not involved with the planning for the P&A of the Well other than in a review capacity.

According to testimony, the Company Man had over 30 years' experience at all levels of the exploration and drilling industry offshore, including some years managing drilling rig operations. Testimony was received that the Company Man was specifically experienced with P&A's, workovers, completions, as well as through tubing-operations using snubbing units, coil tubing, wireline, etc.

While working exclusively for the Operator in the preceding three years, the Company Man supervised a wide range of activities, including those requiring the use of snubbing and coil tubing units, drilling, several workovers and P&A's. The CEM noted that, while contracted to the Operator, the Company Man had been asked to conduct several complex operations according to his experience, without detailed planning instructions. According to testimony, relative freedom of action had been allowed the Company Man to conduct these operations, partly because of a lack of design and engineering personnel, and partly because of the Operator's regard for the Company Man's expertise.

Testimony indicated that neither the Operator's CE nor CEM nor the Company Man had attempted the salvage or P&A of a well inside a bent caisson, as these occurrences have been relatively rare.

From testimony, the CT Contractor is a company that spans several states and has over 25 coil tubing units operating out of more than five districts. The key management personnel of the CTU Contractor all have over 20 years' coil tubing experience, both onshore and offshore, and were part of the startup of this company approximately eight years ago.

The coil tubing unit supplied by the CT Contractor had undergone recent maintenance and was thought to be in excellent working order. Two supervisors were assigned to the MP 98 well work by the CTU Contractor. Both had over 15 years' coil tubing experience and, according to testimony, were considered to be capable and qualified. Testimony was received that the six CTU crewmen assigned to the job were considered qualified to conduct their responsibilities, though with varying degrees of experience.

General Coil Tubing Operations

Description of CT Methods, Equipment, Rig-Up

Coil tubing is simply continuous tubing wrapped around a reel. It can be rapidly lowered into, or raised out of a well because it does not require screwing or unscrewing joints of tubing. The addition of stripping rubbers allows coil tubing to operate within a well under pressure.

Coil tubing is used for many purposes in remedial well operations, a common one being cleaning out sand, debris, or obstructions from inside of a well. To do this, the coil tubing is unreeled into the well to be cleaned out. Different types of fluid can then be circulated down the CT and back up the annulus (the space between the outside of the coil tubing and the inside of the surrounding pipe) to the surface, lifting and removing sand and debris. The use of CT in many circumstances is desirable because of (a) the speed with which it can be lowered into, or pulled out of, the hole; and (b) the ability to operate under varying pressures.

The coiled tubing unit is an assembly of the major equipment components needed to perform a continuous-length tubing service. These basic equipment components usually include a tubing reel, tubing guide, injector head, control console, power supply, and well control stack or BOP Assembly *(see figure 10)*.

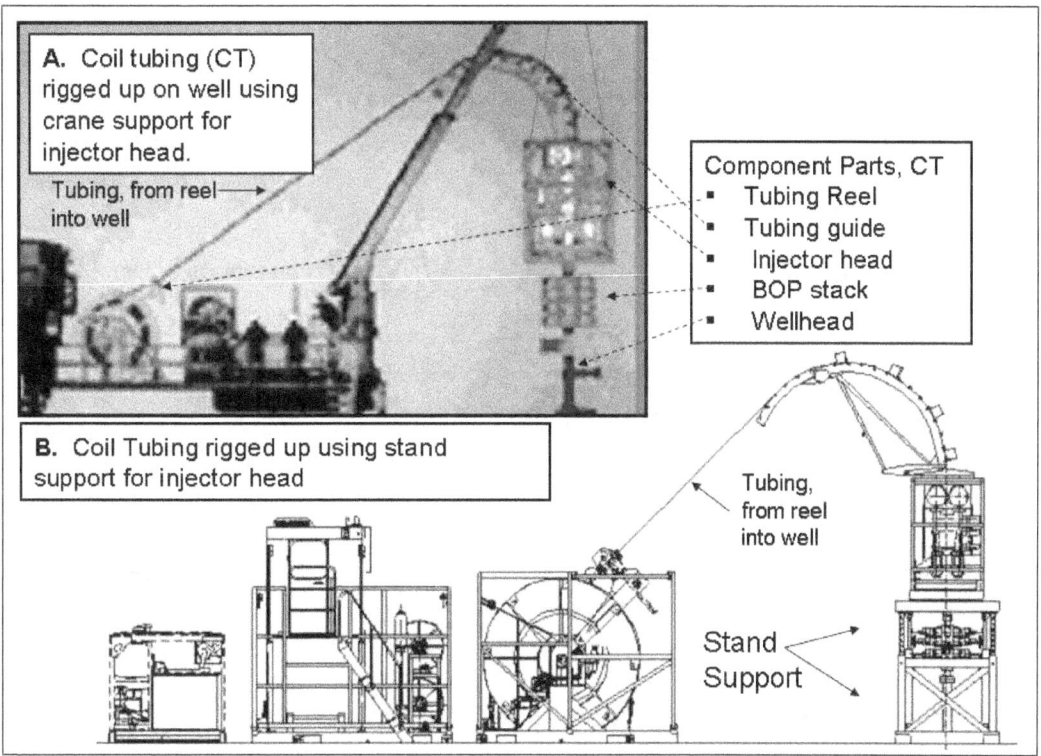

Figure 10: Coil tubing unit components

Coil tubing can be rigged up upon many types of wellheads. By adding a cross-over connection, the base of the coil tubing assembly can be joined to the top of a tree, tubing, drill pipe, casing, or with a special rig up, CT can be inserted into the annulus of casing strings. With proper support equipment, coil tubing can be rigged up high in the air on stuck drill pipe or be situated so that the flexible tubing can access a wellhead considerable distance from the reel. Under special circumstances CT can be used in horizontal wells and within pipelines.

A partial review by the Panel of industry references commonly used for coil tubing operations found that, generally, the focus of these references is on problems encountered when actually operating. The CT Contractor uses a safety manual (the Manual or Safety Manual) as a reference guide to offshore safety for its CTU crews. This Manual is the *Coil Tubing Safety Manual*, by Walter Crow, April 1999 developed under contract 75-97SW41286 prepared for the U. S. Department of Energy (see DOES/SW/41286-1, Distribution Category UC-122).

The Manual references the rig-up of CT in its opening section, 1.0. That section concerns configuration of the well control equipment with two exceptions. Bullet 5 reads in part as follows:

"...Wellheads which have a threaded connections (such as multiple-completions), should consider changing out the tree prior to the coiled tubing workover if at all possible. In the event it is impractical to change out this type of wellhead, two considerations are suggested. First, use a platform-style base to rest the weight of the coiled tubing which will minimize side-loading by the sway of crane support or independent legs..."

The last 'bullet" of section 1.0 reads as follows:

"...High coiled tubing rig ups above the wellhead can translate high bending forces with relatively minor movement from the injector head (even when supported by a crane or platform). A periodic check of the Christmas tree bolts is advisable to insure they have not worked loose during prolonged operations."

Regarding planning of a CTU operation, the Safety Manual, Section 3.1a, reads in part as follows:

"...Conduct a pre-job meeting with the contractor personnel. Determine equipment needs, including any possibilities for contingency operations."

In the Manual, no examples of "high coiled tubing rig ups" are given, nor are any methods of defining such operations, and no method of calculating the bending forces or loads on the supporting equipment is discussed. All visual examples in the Manual show rigging up the CTU on a wellhead by using a flanged connection.

Testimony was received that written guidelines for calculating the loading forces on the connection of the CTU to the wellhead are not generally available. Estimates of the ability of a connection to withstand the weight of the CTU BOP Assembly, injector head, tubing, and operating forces are generally left to the judgment of the operator.

Operation Details

CT Rig-Up Conditions and Factors

The supervisors and managers of the CT Contractor all reported that they had previously encountered similar rig-up conditions to those that existed on the Well; rigging up the CTU atop a 3½-ft joint of 2⅜-in production tubing. However, testimony and subsequent analysis indicated that any such rig-ups directly on a tubing connection were not under the exact circumstances existing on the Lift Boat. Such rig-ups were either conducted onshore with continuous derrick or crane supported equipment stabilized as needed by guyed wires, or were atop products such as drill pipe and large diameter lubricators that were inherently stronger than the 2⅜-in production tubing connection on the Well.

The CT Contractor maintains an engineering office that is available for consultation concerning problems encountered while conducting CTU operations; and the Operator CEM testified that he was available for consultation and was in regular contact with the Company Man onsite. Neither the Operator nor the CT Contractor mentioned any specific company policies defining circumstances when operators in the field were to request engineering support. The CT Contractor engineering office was described as being used primarily as a consulting source during actual operations.

No testimony indicated the CT Contractor engineering office was consulted about bending moments present during rig-up of coil tubing except in cases requiring the coil tubing to span a considerable distance from the reel to the injector head. The Operator CEM did not report being asked to conduct load calculations for any CT rig-ups upon the tie-back tubing string. No calculations of load were included in the Well Plan. No mention of any overt concern about loading while rigging up the CTU or other equipment on the tie-back strings was written into the Well Plan.

According to testimony, the narrow dimensions and layout of the Extension Platform may have made it difficult to use a standard stand support for the injector head to help disperse and stabilize the load, had it been desired. There was no standard way to stabilize the injector head and BOP Assembly by the use of guyed wires because of the narrowness of the Extension Platform.

Specifics, Pre-CTU Rig-Up

Testimony was received regarding the details of the actual rig-up of the CTU on the Well. From that testimony, the CTU Contractor was originally contacted about the P&A of the Well at the beginning of 2005. At that time, the plan called for entering the Well's tubing through the tree without disturbing the position of the Caisson. From the plan of work adopted at that time, this called for a lift boat to be set a distance from the wellhead, in line with the bent Caisson. The coil tubing was then snaked at an angle into the well. It was hoped that the flexibility of the coil tubing would allow it to navigate the bend in the Caisson successfully and allow the well to be cleaned out and P&A'd without straightening the Caisson.

From testimony, the CT Contractor was not chosen to perform this work. Documentation shows that an effort to access the tubing in this manner was attempted by using a different coil tubing company, but during that attempt the coil tubing landed on an obstruction at approximately 10 ft BML in both tubing strings and was unable to be lowered any deeper into the Well. No details of this phase of the P&A were available and it is unknown if the CT employed in this manner was able to circulate or whether an attempt was made to wash the CT deeper.

When the Operator settled on the Plan ultimately employed, no CT service company was involved in the planning process. The CT Contractor was "cold called" directly from the Lift Boat by the Company man and mobilized for the operation after the casing had been successfully cut. According to testimony, the CTU crew and equipment were transported to the Well site on 10-11 August.

Testimony was received that, upon arriving at the site, the CT Contractor supervisors found the Lift Boat had the Extension Platform installed and the tie-back strings attached by overshots to the production tubing. The tie-back strings were landed in 500-lb tension in the slips and had been chained down to the Caisson stub to prevent them from being blown off the wellhead should pressure be encountered while the well was cleaned. However, the 2⅜-in tie-back strings were protruding higher than 30 ft above the Slip Bowl and were already equipped with TIW valves. No stabilization wires were attached to the tie-back strings. No handrails were fitted on the Extension Platform. The Slip Bowl was not secured in the opening in the end of the Extension Platform and openings flanked either side of the Slip Bowl.

Testimony indicates that the CTU equipment for the CT operation was offloaded from the work boat and positioned on the Lift Boat wherever a spot could be found, as the deck of the Lift Boat was crowded. However, room was created for the reel and injector head immediately in front of the temporary work platform. The other equipment was placed where space could be found. It is not known where the BOP Assembly stack was placed on the Lift Boat, but from testimony, no discussion was held about any need to position it in a particular place for a particular type of make up.

Testimony indicates the Company Man wanted the CT Contractor crew to rig up the CTU on top of the unstabilized 2⅜-in tie-back tubing, over 30 ft above the Slip Bowl. According to the CT Contractor personnel, this was not a viable operation because it was thought by both CTU supervisors that the length of the 2⅜-in tie-back tubing could not bear the weight of the CTU assembly without damage, even if the CTU equipment were suspended by a crane.

The CT supervisors recommended adjustments be made to the Extension Platform, Slip Bowls, and the tie-back strings before CT rig-up. These recommendations were accepted by the Company Man and initiated. They were as follows:

1. Re-position the height of the Lift Boat and remove a joint of 2⅜-in tubing from the tie-back string; substitute "pup" joints to get the height of the uppermost collar of both tie-back strings as close as possible to the Slip Bowls.

2. Install hand rails on the temporary work platform.

3. Weld supporting braces on either side of the Slip Bowl to keep it from independently moving around during operations. Testimony was received that the end of the Extension

Platform was swaying slightly from the natural movements of the Lift Boat with the ocean current, wind, and wave action.

Work was begun to accomplish the above recommendations after the equipment was offloaded. The CT Contractor day shift positioned the equipment, checked and prepared it for operations. The CT Contractor supervisors continued to consult with the Company Man on the layout of the False Rotary while preparing the CTU equipment.

According to testimony, the re-positioning of the Lift Boat and the shortening of the tie-back tubing extending above the Slip Bowl was completed by about 1600 hrs. The final length of both strings of the 2⅜-in tie-back tubing extending above the Slip bowl was approximately 3.5 ft. Atop both tie-back strings, a 22-in long TIW valve was installed. According to testimony, the TIW valve has a wide central cross-section containing the actual valve mechanisms. The tie-back strings were spaced out in such a way that the wide portions of the two TIW valves were partially opposed to each other rather than staggered.

Testimony indicates that the slips could not be gotten closer to the uppermost 2⅜-in collars because the interference of the TIW valve cross-sections would cause the axes of the tie-back strings to be progressively angled farther from the vertical, the closer the slips were to the collars. This would result in the BOP Assembly being made up and orientated at a progressively greater angle from the vertical, rather than centered on the tie-back string, the closer the slips were to the tie-back tubing end connections.

The Company Man testified that some two weeks before the CTU was mobilized, a CT contractor representative visited the Lift Boat and observed the conditions in which the CTU would be operating. No documents were received that confirm this account and the physical work environment existing on the Lift Boat at the time is unknown. The CT Contactor personnel were unable to confirm or deny the visit but had no record of any recommendations received from any such visit. The Company Man also testified that the original extended height of the tie-back strings above the Slip Bowl was not intended to be the rig-up height of the coil tubing. He testified that hand rails were previously installed on the temporary work deck Extension Platform but had been removed so unspecified tasks could be performed.

Specifics, Rig-Up, JSA Meeting

After the arrival of the CTU and crew onto the Lift Boat, the night shift of the CTU retired and the day shift prepared the CTU unit for service and assisted in the changes in the geography of the Extension Platform.

Testimony was received from the Company Man that he held a fully attended JSA meeting and discussed the plan to make up the entire CTU wellhead unit, including the BOP Assembly and the injector head (the Wellhead Unit), on the deck prior to lifting any part of it onto the tie-back string. The Company Man also testified that he separately instructed the crane operator and the CTU night shift supervisor that the Wellhead Unit be made up and hoisted in one lift, keeping the crane attached at all times. The Operator CEM testified that he was under the impression that a single lift of the entire Wellhead Unit was contemplated, but he could not recall when that was discussed. Differing testimony was received from the crane operator and CTU night supervisor.

After being told to rig up, the night supervisor testified he conducted the operation in a conventional manner, separately installing the cross-over sub, the gate valve, the chicksan flow return piping and assembly and the BOP Assembly and stack in separate lifts, making each component up to those already installed. The Company Man had retired after initially telling the night supervisor to rig up the CTU.

Documentation indicates that on 11 August 2005, according to an Operator JSA form, the Company Man conducted a safety meeting to review the upcoming operation. The subjects covered in the meeting as listed on the sign-in sheet were as follows:

1) Use a work vest and a required fall protection lanyard if working 6 ft or higher above the work platform (Extension Platform) and no smoking allowed on the bow of the boat;

(2) Instructions were given for the actual test pressure to be used for the wireline lubricator;

(3) The objective of the wireline operation was defined to be the location of the position of the SCSSV's;

(4) Instructions were given for the pressure test of the CTU lines and the packoff overshots;

(5) The procedure to be followed by wireline and CTU (if the tie-back string packoffs were successfully tested) was outlined.

Those in attendance signed the form. The list of those who signed the JSA form did not contain the signature of the CTU night shift supervisor, nor any of the CTU night shift crew. Nor did it contain the signature of the night crane operator. Personnel from the CTU night shift and the crane operator testified that they did not attend a Company Man-conducted JSA meeting. The CTU night shift supervisor stated that the rig-up procedure for the CTU was not discussed with him formally or informally. The crane operator reported he began the operation without knowledge of what was being attempted.

In section 37.0 of the Operator's Safety Manual, guidelines are given as to the Operator's requirements for pre-job safety meetings. The Operator's manual reads in part as follows:

"*Job Safety Analysis (JSA)*
"*...a JSA will be required for, but not limited to the following jobs: ...*
- *Jobs requiring personnel to work at heights requiring fall protection...*
- *Crane operations involving critical or heavy lifts..."*

"*Responsibilities*
"*The JSA is a group activity coordinated by the supervisor. All personnel including contractors involved with the project must be involved in the Job Safety Analysis process. He or she will ensure that the following is observed:*

- *The sequence of job steps is reviewed*
- *Hazards are identified*
- *Necessary safeguards are determined*
- *The assigning of responsible individuals*
- *The completion of the Forest JSA form."*

The CTU day shift supervisor testified that he discussed the rig-up of the CTU with the Company Man. He testified that he recommended that the BOP Assembly and the injector head be made up into one lift unit on the deck of the Lift Boat. He was unsure of the location of the BOP stack on the Lift Boat prior to initiating CTU rig-up.

Specifics, CTU Operational Details

When the re-positioning of the Lift Boat, spacing out the tie-back strings, and additional alteration of the work environment on the Extension Platform were completed at approximately 1800 hrs, the CTU shift change occurred. At that time, the wireline contractors were beginning to conduct their operations. According to testimony, the CTU night shift conducted some maintenance operations and looked over the equipment needed to begin CTU operations. The CTU day shift supervisor testified he and his shift went off tower and prepared to eat and retire.

Both the CTU supervisors testified that they had no discussion of how to rig up the CTU BOP Assembly and the injector head at shift change. Testimony was received that a shift change meeting between the supervisors is a usual practice. However, it is not a required or a defined part of the CT Contractor or Operator manuals. In this case, no such meeting was held and testimony was received that the timing of operations was a contributing factor. The night shift came on duty while other operations were ongoing. By the time the CTU rig-up was ordered, the day shift, including the supervisor, had retired.

The CTU night supervisor testified he received no instructions of any special considerations to be followed during rig-up of the CTU. The Company Man told him to "rig-up" at approximately 2130 hrs with no other discussion. Testimony and documentation indicate that the CTU night supervisor held a JSA meeting with his shift crew and discussed the operation as he understood it. The crane operator did not attend this JSA meeting. The CT Contractor's JSA form was completed with the signatures of all the CT Contractor night shift. The safety topics covered in that meeting as listed included testing, rigging up, stabbing pipe, flanging up the BOP's, and filling the reel. Special or unique methods for rigging up the CTU were not included as a topic for discussion in the meeting.

Testimony was received that, in order to make up the BOP Assembly and the injector head as a single lift unit (the Wellhead Unit) prior to hoisting it onto the tie back tubing, the CTU BOP Assembly must be positioned directly in front of the injector head and a certain crane procedure followed. The position of the BOP Assembly prior to initiating the CTU rig-up operation was not positively identified by testimony. However, some indication was received that it was possibly not pre-positioned for Wellhead Unit makeup because of the crowded nature of the Lift Boat deck. It was reported that rearranging the equipment on the deck was possibly necessary before the Wellhead Unit could have been made up prior to positioning it on the tubing.

When the BOP Assembly was fully made up on top of the tie-back tubing, it is reported that the weight of all the components, including the chicksan flowline attached on the starboard outboard side of the BOP's, was approximately 3,000 lbs. The center of gravity of the BOP Assembly was estimated to be 10.5 – 11.5 ft above the slips in the Slip Bowl *(see figure 8 for data)*.

Testimony was received that the BOP Assembly stayed atop the 2⅜-in tie-back string for several minutes after the crane was detached and while the CT Tech was working on the lift cap. Testimony indicated that, immediately prior to the rapid canting of the BOP Assembly to starboard, the crane was swinging into position to lift the 7,000-lb injector head to be installed atop the BOP Assembly. Testimony was also received that a vibration was felt on the Extension Platform. Subsequently, the BOP Assembly began to sway slightly prior to the failure of the tubing supporting the BOP Assembly.

Panel members conducted conversations with professional structural engineers about the failure of the 2⅜-in N-80 4.6 lbs/ft schedule B tie-back tubing and the torque necessary to cause that failure. These conversations yielded a consensus opinion that minimum yield in the schedule B pipe steel, absent any structural flaws, should be between 30 KSI and 45 KSI and once the yield was reached, plastic deformation would take place followed by failure. Assuming static conditions, opinions were received that a torque loading of approximately 2,800 to 3,800 ft-lbs could have created plastic modulus, leading to failure in 2⅜-in tubing. If movement of the load applying the torque occurred, opinions were received that a change in load orientation from axial compression to dynamic cantilever loading could have occurred with corresponding failure at equivalent lower static torque ratings.

Using the data available *(see figure 8)*, the calculated axial load on the tubing was between 3,000 and 3,500 lbs with the center of gravity estimated to be approximately 11 ft above the point where the 2⅜-in tie-back string was held in the slips. In this case, a static displacement of the center of gravity of the BOP Assembly of less than 1 ft could have resulted in plastic deformation and failure of the 2⅜-in tie-back. Any addition of a momentum force caused by movement of the load could have effectively added to the static load torque, or changed the torque effect to a dynamic modulus.

Other factors were discussed that could have transferred torque from the BOP Assembly to the 2⅜-inch tie-back tubing. These included the following: (1) the possibility that the BOP Assembly was initially rigged up at a slight angle because of the displacement caused by the TIW valves; and (2) the return chicksan line hanging off the starboard side of the BOP stack could have added side loading.

As previously noted, testimony was received that the BOP Assembly swayed and was in some degree of motion immediately prior to failure. A discussion of possible causes for the motion of the BOP's noted that motion could have been induced from several possible causes or a combination of them. Possible causes discussed included the following: (a) the natural movement/sway of the lift boat; (b) the harmonics of wave and current action on the tie-back string extending from the False Rotary to the overshot, approximately 120 ft; (c) other outside causation such as an unreported collision between supply boat and Lift Boat; (d) the movement induced into the system by the rotation of the crane.

Revised Detailed CT Plan Submitted After the Accident

After the accident, the CT Contractor submitted a detailed well plan of action to continue operations while preventing re-occurrence of the previous failure. This proposal differed from the procedure that led to the Accident in the following way:

- The Wellhead Unit was to be made up on deck into a single lift before hoisting onto the tubing;

- To do this, the BOP skid was to be pre-located so that makeup of the Wellhead Unit for a single lift could be accomplished;

- A support platform was to be installed beneath the injector head with the legs on the Extension Platform;

- The entire structure was to be chained to the Extension Platform to provide stability and the crane was to remain continuously attached during operations;

- The second crane was to be positioned so that its hook could be used as fall protection.

29

Conclusions

The Accident

After a review of the information obtained during the investigation, it is concluded that, at approximately 0012 hours on 12 August 2005, while operations were being conducted to rig-up coil tubing, a joint of 2⅜-in tubing supporting the BOP stack assembly bent suddenly at a 90-degree angle under the load. The bending of the tubing caused the BOP Assembly to break free and fall overboard. A CT technician was attached to the BOP Assembly by his safety line and was pulled overboard by the weight of the BOP Assembly, causing his death.

Cause of Fatality

1. *Lack of engineering calculations* – The CT BOP Assembly was rigged up atop the 2⅜-in tie-back tubing joint without any other support. It is concluded that no engineering calculations determined the ability of the 2⅜-in tubing to hold the BOP Assembly load under the operational conditions that existed on the job site.

2. *Inadequate physical work environment* – It is concluded that the temporary work platform created on the Lift Boat to conduct operations provided no easily accessible methods of affixing fall protection safety lines other than to the BOP stack.

3. *Lack of detailed planning and review during preparation of the well plan* – It is concluded that the planning for the operation failed to consider certain operational details related to the Extension Platform and the unusual 2⅜-in tie-back tubing connection.

- The difficulties of rigging up CT that were inherent in the plan adopted by Operator were not identified or recognized during the planning and review process, as the written plan stated only "rig up coil tubing" with no discussion or caution of unusual circumstances.

- The CT Contractor was not included in the planning process. The unusual nature of the work platform and the 2⅜-in tie-back string connection was not made apparent to the CT Contractor until the crew and equipment arrived on site.

4. *Insufficient onsite pre-job review and communication* – It is concluded that the onsite job preview was not sufficient to prepare adequately for the CT rig-up operation.

- No JSA meeting discussing rig-up procedure for the coil tubing and attended by all relevant personnel was held by the Operator's representative.
- No shift hand-off meeting between CT Contractor shift supervisors addressed problems or methods of rigging up the coil tubing.

5. *Insufficient onsite oversight* – No oversight of the CT rig-up process was given by the Operator's representative. Therefore, no mention of an alternative method of rigging up, if contemplated, was made to the CT personnel on duty when rig-up was initiated.

Probable Contributing Cause of the Fatality

1. *Probable lack of clear guidelines requiring field operatives to seek engineering consultation* – It is probable that the lack of clear Operator and CT Contractor guidelines specifying when field operations should request engineering review of rig-up operations placed the responsibility of recognizing potential mechanical problems on the field operations personnel.

2. *Probable incomplete analysis and communication during planning and operations* – It is probable that the failure to analyze completely the operational rig-up during the planning phase and communicate the details contributed to the occurrence of the accident. This failure probably extended throughout the CT Contractor and the Operator's organizations. The conditions actually encountered during the rig-up were probably not known to the onshore support elements of either CT Contractor or Operator, and these conditions probably differed significantly from those previously encountered in the experience of all involved.

Possible Contributing Causes of the Fatality

1. *Possible supervisor lack of experience or unrealistic problem solving expectations* – It is possible that the onsite Operator's representative was lacking in experience needed to supervise such an unusual operational plan, or that management expectations of his ability to solve any operational problems were not realistic.

- The initial instruction to the CT Contractor personnel to rig-up on top of >30 ft of 2 3/8-in tubing was not inherently reasonable or possible.

- The unsubstantial hand rails on the extension deck, the openings in the deck surrounding the false rotary, and the lack of rigid fall protection points on the extension deck were oversights that possibly should have been addressed prior to initiating any operations.

- The failure to conduct a fully attended JSA meeting dealing with all potential problems before initiating the CT rig-up was not according to recommended practice or Operator policy.

- The failure of the Operator's representative to be present, review the conditions immediately prior to beginning rig-up of the CT, and to correct the methodology if a different way of conducting the operation were contemplated, was possibly an oversight.

2. *Possible failure of Operator's planning and review process caused by complexity or lack of explicit experience* – It is possible Operator personnel in the planning and review process failed to anticipate operational problems created by the unusual work plan, either because of lack of specific experience or because the plan itself was overly complex.

3. *Possible lack of references and information in the Field Manual* –It is possible that the failure of the *Coil Tubing Safety Manual* to detail the conditions that require additional load support when rigging up on top of small tubulars was a contributing factor. The Manual gives only superficial guidance to be aware of possible bending forces created by "high coiled tubing rig-ups" and does not provide specifics useful in the field to judge the need for auxiliary support.

Recommendations

It is recommended that MMS issue a Safety Alert that briefly describes the fatal accident and that alerts the operators to three subjects as follows:

1. *Operators and contractors should be aware of the dangers inherent in rigging up unsupported CT elements on top of tubulars. When in doubt or when faced with unusual situations, engineering calculations should be sought.*

2. *The Operators should review their planning process to ensure a detailed review of every element by fully experienced personnel if a unique or unusual operation is contemplated. Operators should consider including specialty contractors in the planning process for unique and unusual operations.*

3. *Operators should ensure offshore supervision is fully qualified for any contemplated unusual operations. Operators and contractors should ensure that the details of all plans are fully communicated to all parties and shifts by using JSA and pre-job shift hand-off meetings.*

It is also recommended that the MMS consider a study to (1) examine the possibility of a creating a field method of identifying bending forces for various tubular products, and (2) determine if a need exists to introduce related regulations requiring such calculations before operations commence.

www.ingramcontent.com/pod-product-compliance
Lightning Source LLC
Chambersburg PA
CBHW080733290526
45790CB00008B/3168